12 GREAT TIPS ON
WRITING A BLOG

by Barbara Krasner

www.12StoryLibrary.com

12-Story Library is an imprint of Peterson Publishing Company and Press Room Editions.

Produced for 12-Story Library by Red Line Editorial

Photographs ©: pixdeluxe/iStockphoto, cover, 1; Syda Productions/Shutterstock Images, 4; Susan Schmitz/Shutterstock Images, 5; Antonio Diaz/Shutterstock Images, 6; Orange Line Media/Shutterstock Images, 7; conejota/Shutterstock Images, 8; Amy Keen/Shutterstock Images, 9; Purestock/Thinkstock, 10; Merrydolla/Shutterstock Images, 11; Creativa Images/Shutterstock Images, 12; wavebreakmedia/Shutterstock Images, 13; ymgerman/Shutterstock Images, 14; Niloo/Shutterstock Images, 15; ProQuest Database, 16; RTimages/Shutterstock Images, 17; K2 PhotoStudio/Shutterstock Images, 18; vgajic/iStockphoto, 19; Yuri/iStockphoto, 20; Samuel Borges Photography/Shutterstock Images, 21, 28; Julian Rovagnati/Shutterstock Images, 22; Mark Bowden/iStock/Thinkstock, 23, 29; Pixsooz/Shutterstock Images, 24; Monkey Business Images/Shutterstock Images, 26; Julius Kielaitis/Shutterstock Images, 27

Library of Congress Cataloging-in-Publication Data
Names: Krasner, Barbara.
Title: 12 great tips on writing a blog / by Barbara Krasner.
Other titles: Twelve great tips on writing a blog
Description: Mankato, MN : 12-Story Library, 2017. | Includes bibliographical
   references and index.
Identifiers: LCCN 2016002319 (print) | LCCN 2016005610 (ebook) | ISBN
   9781632352736 (library bound : alk. paper) | ISBN 9781632353238 (pbk. :
   alk. paper) | ISBN 9781621434412 (hosted ebook)
Subjects: LCSH: Blogs--Juvenile literature. | Online journalism--Juvenile
   literature.
Classification: LCC TK5105.8884 .K84 2016 (print) | LCC TK5105.8884 (ebook) |
   DDC 070.5/79734--dc23
LC record available at http://lccn.loc.gov/2016002319

Printed in the United States of America
Mankato, MN
May, 2016

Access free, up-to-date content on this topic plus a full digital version of this book. Scan the QR code on page 31 or use your school's login at 12StoryLibrary.com.

Table of Contents

1

Have a Purpose

Congratulations! You've decided to join the blogosphere with your very own blog. The word *blog* is short for weblog. A blog is a website in which you record, or log, your thoughts, stories, and experiences. Your blog can help you talk with people who are interested in the same things as you, no matter where they live.

The first thing to do when starting a blog is to find a subject to blog about. To help you pick a subject, read other blogs. Which ones catch your interest? How might you offer a different perspective on a subject? Keep in mind, the more focused your subject, the more you will attract followers who share your passion.

Let's say you love animals and your family often fosters litters. A blog about animals may be too broad. A blog about caring for newborn puppies and kittens might be specific enough.

Or maybe you have a particular service goal in mind. Perhaps you've started a neighborhood campaign

Blog about something you love or are interested in.

to save the old oak tree. A blog can help you make people aware of your efforts. It may help you gain support.

Your blog will contain posts and pages. Pages can include information you don't change often, such as an About Me page. An About Me page is where you can tell your readers about yourself. This can help them get to know you. Be careful, though, not to put private information online, such as your phone number or address. Posts are what you write on a regular basis. They include the content you create about your subject.

Your posts can take many forms. You can make lists of tips. You can share current events. You can review books about your subject. You can recommend products. You might even have other people contribute their thoughts in guest posts.

Some people blog about raising their pets.

TRY IT OUT

List three possible subjects for your blog. Does one give you more energy than the others? Come up with a name for your blog that captures your passion.

Quick Tips

- Choose a blog subject you're interested in.
- Read other blogs like the one you want to create.
- Decide on the types of blog posts you'll use.

Know Your Audience

You've now decided on your blog's subject. Before you start writing your first post, think about the people you want to write for. Are your readers looking for a formal style of writing? Formal writing follows all of the rules of grammar and word usage. Conversational style is less formal. It sounds more like how you would talk with your friends. In general, blogs tend to use a more informal tone than other kinds of writing, such as newspaper articles.

To learn about your audience, do some research. Type into a search engine a few keywords connected with your subject. Make sure you include the word *blog*. That should produce a listing of blogs. Check out

People tend to talk more informally with their friends.

a few of them. What kind of tone do the posts have? Is the writing formal or informal?

Suppose your subject is caring for newborn kittens. You may come across many personal blogs on this subject. Posts on these sites might include photos of newborn kittens. The writing is probably informal. The blogs are likely based on their authors' experiences. Your keyword search might bring up other results. Some might be organizations, such as WebMD and PetFirst Pet Insurance. These take a more formal tone. Chances are, the audience for the blogs you come across are people who adopt pets or whose pets deliver litters. The audiences for the more formal websites are likely people searching for expert answers to problems.

By looking at other sites, you can learn more about who will read your own content. You can take cues from these sites about what kind of tone to use on your blog.

Check out how other people blog about your topic.

Plan Your Posts

A successful blog takes time and effort. Some experts believe a blogger needs to post several times a day to quickly gain readers. But many people post less often. Only you can decide how much time you can give your blog. Whatever you decide, it's best to have a plan from the start.

You might choose to blog only once a week. Or you could decide to blog every day. In either case, you should develop a schedule for your posts.

This makes it easier for others to know when to visit your blog. Remember, your goal is to deliver great content to your readers.

Let's say you want to write a blog about pirates. You could post reviews of books or articles about pirates on Tuesdays. You could post interviews with people, including authors or experts, on Thursdays. This scheduling sets up your

Be sure to make a realistic schedule for your blog.

Quick Tips

- Decide how much time you want to give to your blogging project.
- Set up a regular writing and publishing schedule.
- Make sure you can stick to your schedule.

audience's expectations for your blog. They'll be excited for your reviews on Tuesdays and your interviews on Thursdays. The schedule also

SAMPLE SCHEDULE

Week 1: Tuesday: book review of *Jean Laffite: The Pirate Who Saved America*; Thursday: e-mail interview with author Susan Goldman Rubin

Week 2: Tuesday: book review of *Treasure Island*; Thursday: interview with local children's librarian

Week 3: Tuesday, book review of *The Ultimate Pirate Handbook*; Thursday: interview with local university history professor

Week 4: Tuesday, a roundup of the new pirate books published this month; Thursday: interview with a staff member from a pirate museum

makes it easier for you. But be sure your schedule works for you. The Internet has many blogs that have been abandoned. Don't let one of them be yours!

Record audio from interviews with a voice recorder.

Identify Keywords

How can you attract readers to your blog? Think about how you search for new blogs to read. You probably enter a few search terms into a search engine. Your potential followers will do the same to try to find your blog. Make it easy for them by focusing on keywords.

Make a list of keywords that people might use to find information on your subject. Use those words in your posts. Blogging platforms often offer you a way to highlight keywords. Popular blogging platforms for kids include Kidzworld or Yoursphere.

Your subject probably has its own set of unique words. Keywords about pirates could include Blackbeard, Jean Laffite, *Treasure Island*, pirate ship, buried treasure, pirate bounty, or treasure map. It's also a good idea to include a place with your

People use search terms to find what they are looking for online.

KEYWORDS

Picking good keywords will help attract more people to your blog. Notice the keywords in this section of a pirate blog post:

Aarghh! 5 Tips for Reading Treasure Maps

Ahoy, ye mateys! You've found a **treasure map from the Caribbean**, have ye? Not sure what to do with it? Here are five of my tips for figuring out what the map says:

1. Look for the X that marks the spot of the **buried treasure**.

2. Look for the map's legend and scale. This will tell you how many paces you must walk to find your **pirate bounty**.

> Keywords, such as *buried treasure*, describe things specific to your subject so others can find your blog.

keywords, such as "Caribbean buried treasure" or "East Coast pirate ships." The purpose of using keywords in your content is for a search engine to find a match between your blog and someone's search. When you include a word that describes a location, this will allow people looking for that exact information to find you. You can enter these keywords for yourself and see what blogs and websites come up. The results could give you some ideas for more blog posts.

Quick Tips

- Make a list of keywords people might use to find information on your subject.
- Test your list by conducting a web search of your own.
- Include keywords in your blog posts.

Give Away Your Knowledge

You've chosen a subject you like to write and talk about. You know a lot about your subject. It may sound strange to give away your knowledge, but it's the way for you to increase your readership. Share what you know. Show that you are an authority on your subject. Post consistently and often. Your audience will come to expect your posts. And they will soon start to trust your knowledge.

But maybe you aren't sure about what you really know. Do you read a lot about sports and play on a team? Do you watch a lot of movies? Do you deal with a particular physical challenge? Are you devoted to a social cause? Even if you are an expert, you still need to do research to support your statements. It's always a good idea

Doing research can help make you more of an expert on your topic.

to let your readers know where you got your information. If you've used a book for your research, share the author and title. If you used a website, share the name of it with a link.

Research allows you to confidently talk about other subjects on your blog. It also shows your readers that you are committed to good content.

Statistics on your site will tell you whether your readers value your knowledge. For example, if ten people visit your site every time you post, then you know they want your content. Keep thinking of ways to give them more of what they want!

Quick Tips

- Think of ways to give your knowledge away for free from your blog.
- Tell your readers about the sources you've used for your research.
- Share consistently and frequently.

TRY IT OUT

What do you know more about than your friends do? What knowledge do people compliment you on? Sports? Books? Video games? Nature? Animals? History? Make a list. They could be future blogging opportunities.

Write Catchy Headlines

Experts say that when people are online, they read differently. They first scan the page. If nothing catches their attention, readers will jump to something else. This means headlines are very important. Consider a blog post's headline a writing project of its own. It has a big job to do. It must draw in your audience. It must communicate the whole idea of your post simply and effectively.

Headlines serve another purpose, too. When potential readers use search engines, headlines come up in the search results. Your reader may look no further than the headline. But if your headline is constructed well, that person will decide to click ahead to your blog post.

People who work at magazines have known for many years how to write

Readers can jump to many different things when reading online.

Magazines draw readers' attention with catchy headlines.

Quick Tips

- Think of your post's headline as a separate writing project.
- Write a headline that includes keywords and a benefit to the reader.
- Write your headline as if it has to stand on its own.

a headline that gets people to buy their magazines. Their rules also apply to blog headlines. Readers scan headlines to find something of value to them. You must therefore think about how your information benefits your readers. A headline with a number easily communicates value. Keep the headline short enough to be interesting but long enough to carry meaning.

SAMPLE HEADLINES

Good headlines grab readers' interest. A good headline may be the difference between someone visiting or not visiting your blog. Here are some examples of headlines that make readers want to learn more:

10 Ways to Attract an Audience to Your Blog
5 Organizations You Can Contact Now to Support Your Cause
Town Mayor Accepts Petition to Save Oak Tree
5 Tips for Keeping a Newborn Kitten Healthy
How to Find Buried Treasure along the Atlantic Coast
Author Susan Goldman Rubin Speaks Out about Pirates

15

Use
White Space

When it comes web content, many people first survey the page before reading. It is not a good idea to present your content in a solid block of text. You might wear out your readers before they start reading. They won't know where to focus.

White space gives eyes a rest. White space is visual separation. It keeps us from becoming overwhelmed by what appears on the screen or page. When you write your blog post, you are also creating your readers' experience. Guide them through your post. Think about how they will view it. Put your writing into paragraphs and bulleted lists. Use subheadings to break up the text. Subheadings can also help you transition from one subject to another. You want your readers to view your post as a

For many years, it was normal for newspapers to not use much white space.

DAILY NEWS

World - Business - Finance - Lifestyle - Travel - Sport - Weather

Issue: 240104

First Edition

THE WORLDS BEST SELLING NATIONAL NEWSPAPER

Est - 1965

Monday 5th June

World leaders meet in London to discuss the global economy.

THE INSIDE STORY

Have scientists made a major breakthrough in the never ending search for a cure?

Read the full story on - Page 3

Can you live without technology, discover how comp...

Climate chan... recycling r... difference ... just repeati...

well-made piece of content, not one you just threw together at the last minute.

The key is to write in short blocks of information. Keep your sentence length short, too. A good rule is no more than 20 words in a sentence.

WRITING WITH WHITE SPACE

Break up your writing into short blocks:

5 Groups You Can Contact Now to Support Your Cause

I've spent the last three months working to save the oak tree in our town square. I found five groups to help me. Maybe they can help you, too.

Group #1: Chamber of Commerce

Your local chamber of commerce is a good choice because:

- Its members live in the town.
- People know and respect its members.
- They have meetings where you can state your cause.

Quick Tips

- Break up your blocks of content to create white space.
- Use subheadings.
- Use paragraphs.
- Use bulleted lists.

Pictures Say 1,000 Words

You have your blog post topic. You've written a snappy headline. You've arranged your text in a visually appealing way with subheadings, paragraphs, and bulleted lists. Now it's time to think of images.

Photos spice up your text. They set your content apart. With every post, think about how you can add photos to make your content better. If you've done an interview, ask the person you interviewed to send you a photo. Or use your own photos. That way you don't have to worry about asking permission to use others'. Just be

sure to talk to a parent or other adult before posting any photos of yourself online.

Videos make your blog more interesting. They also keep your readers on your site longer. You can use your own videos. You can also check out online sources to see if any there are any videos of your

Some bloggers share photos of things they've made.

Quick Tips

- Use photos to enhance your blog post.
- Embed videos related to your post.
- Give credit when you use others' material.

TRY IT OUT

What types of images could you use on your blog? Are there videos you could link to? List three kinds of images and three kinds of videos you could use. Remember that some can belong to you.

subject. Then, follow the instructions for your blogging platform to embed the video in your blog post.

Video is best when it shows action, such as someone exploring a ship. If the video is just someone talking, it may be of little value to your blog.

Keep your video short, no longer than one minute. You want your reader to stay on your page. If the video is long, the viewer might get bored and leave your blog. If you pick your images and video carefully, your readers will remember not just your words but also your great images.

Videos let readers engage in your site in a different way.

Include Links

You can help your blog gain popularity by linking to other websites and blogs. On a blog, links are usually words or photos. When readers click on links, they are taken to other websites. If these sites are blogs, their owners may also link to your site. Linking helps grow your blog's content by connecting it to other content. It can also help you find more readers.

Studies have shown our eyes are drawn to links. Usually they are underlined. This makes them stand out on the page. To make the most of your links, create the link from descriptive text. For example, instead of linking the words *click here*, link the words *article on buried*

treasure. You'll want to link to well-respected sites. Government sites are a good option. Their addresses end in *.gov*. School sites are also good. They end in *.edu*. Sites like these

> When people click on a link, they are taken to content on a different page.

Link to sites you think your readers will enjoy.

will give your blog credibility. And the more good websites you refer your readers to, the more comfortable they will feel clicking your links.

You should also link to your own posts. Doing this helps readers find information quickly and easily. They then won't have to search for it through your search box or through your blog's archive.

Avoid linking from your first paragraph. You want readers to start reading your blog post before moving to another page.

Quick Tips

- Include helpful links to other blogs and websites.
- Link text in new blog posts to your past posts.
- Use descriptive phrases in your links.

LINKING

In the following paragraph, underlined words represent links. As you read, think of where the text might link to. Is it easy to tell?

In a past blog post about <u>Florida buried treasure</u>, I interviewed Florida International University expert <u>Dr. X. Markus Spot</u>. I spoke to him about his <u>Atlantic reef research</u>. He said, "History has shown that many shipwrecks lie among the Atlantic reefs. How much gold is on the ocean floor, we just don't know."

Keep It Short

How long should your blog post be? Most blog posts run about 400 to 800 words. When you include photos and videos, you can get away with less text. Your goal is to present as much interesting content as possible. But you also want to give out your information in chunks that readers can handle. With too little information, readers will not feel like your post is worth their time. With too much information, readers might not have time to get through it all.

If your post gets too long, you can separate it into shorter parts. Each part might end up as its own post. You can even create a series on the same topic. For example, let's say you've spoken with some experts and you have a list of ten traits that pirates share. To write up

Readers can lose interest if blog posts are too long.

Quick Tips

- Count the number of words you write for your blog post.
- If it's too long, make a new post with the extra writing.
- Be sure to include photos and videos to make your post more interesting.

TRY IT OUT

Pick a paragraph of your own writing. Look for ways to get rid of words you don't need. See if you can replace two words with one.

all ten in one post would make the post too long. You could instead write two posts, "Experts Name Five Common Traits among Pirates" and

"Five More Things Pirates Have in Common."

Before you post your content, think about its length. Is your post as short as it can be? Do you say the same thing more than once? Have you added photos or videos to enhance your content?

If there is too much information, split posts up.

23

Review and Edit

You've written your blog post, found photos and videos, and decided what you'll link to. You're all ready to publish, right? Not quite yet.

All writers must check their content. You must make sure the writing is clear. You should proofread each word, sentence, paragraph, and page. Is every word spelled correctly? Is proper punctuation used throughout? Use your computer's word processing program to spell-check your writing.

Also, check your main headline and your subheadings. Do all the

Making sure your writing is error free is important whether you are writing on your blog or for a class.

REVISION

Notice the changes proofreading can make in part of a blog post:

10 Shore-Fire Ways to Find ~~Bureid~~ Buried Treasure

Ahoy mateys! I'm ~~shore~~ sure you're wondering about the best ways to find buried treasure in the ~~Untied States~~ United States' Atlantic coast. I've asked a few experts to share ~~they're~~ their tips here.

Tip 1: ~~conduct~~ Conduct research on ~~ship wrecks~~ shipwrecks.

Professor X. Markus Spot of ~~The University of Florida~~ Florida International University suggests you learn where the shipwrecks are along the seacoast. His recent book, *The Treasure Hunter's Guide,* is a good place to start.

headlines pack a punch? Are they inviting the blog visitor to read more? Have you used bulleted lists? Does the page look attractive?

Quick Tips

- Make sure your writing is clear.
- Proofread each blog post for proper spelling and grammar.
- Use your word processing program's spell-check feature.
- Ask a friend or adult to look over your content.

A poorly edited blog post can make a reader decide not to come back. When there are mistakes, it looks like the author doesn't care about the blog. Readers want to feel like the things they are reading are important, especially to the writer.

You may want to ask a friend or adult to look over your writing for you. Sometimes it's difficult to find your own errors. When you're ready, go ahead and publish your post. You've done it!

Engage Your Audience

A successful blog is not based on how many followers you have. Instead, success is based on how your readers interact with your information. Great content will keep them coming back for more.

Blogs have features that allow the writer to interact with his or her followers. One of these features is the ability to poll. You can ask readers questions with this feature. You can also ask questions at the bottom of your blog post, asking for feedback. For example, you could ask, "Has the situation I've described in this blog post ever happened to you?" You can ask for feedback on your content or your blog's design.

You should reply to every comment you receive on your

Blogs can be places where people interact online.

facebook

Connect with friends and the world around you on Facebook.

Social media sites can help you gain more readers.

blog. That allows you to keep the conversation going. At the very least, you can thank the person for commenting. If a reader posts a disrespectful comment, acknowledge that person's right to his or her opinion. You might also ask questions to find out why that person has this opinion.

Once you find an online community, engage in it. Let experts know about your blog. They can help get the word out. Mention them in your posts. Have others write posts for your blog. Write posts for others' blogs. Read and comment on blogs similar to yours. Mention other bloggers' posts in your own posts and link to them. Share your blog on social media. Most blogging platforms allow you to publish your posts to social media sites. All of these things can help build a strong community and bring readers to your blog.

Quick Tips

- Learn the features of your blogging platform.
- Respond to comments and questions your readers post.
- Ask questions.
- Invite guests to write posts for your blog.
- Share your posts through social media.

TRY IT OUT

Write down four ways you can build a stronger online community around your blog.

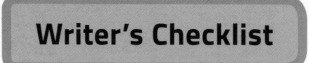

Writer's Checklist

✓ Find a blog subject you're passionate about.

✓ Determine who will read your blog posts.

✓ Set up a realistic writing and publishing schedule.

✓ Make a list of keywords for each blog post.

✓ Identify and write about your special areas of knowledge.

✓ Write brief headlines that use keywords and offer value to your readers.

✓ Use headlines, subheadings, paragraphs, and bulleted lists.

✓ Increase the appeal of your posts with photos and videos.

✓ Link your posts to previous posts and other sites.

✓ Write briefly and clearly.

✓ Review and edit your posts before publishing.

✓ Engage with your audience through comments and polls.

Glossary

archive
Older content that is stored.

blogging platform
A system that allows you to set up and publish a blog.

blogosphere
The online world of personal websites and blogs.

content
The text, photos, links, and other information on a website.

embed
To include or incorporate.

follower
Someone who subscribes to or pays attention to a website.

keywords
A set of carefully chosen words for search engines to recognize.

poll
To conduct a survey.

search box
A field on a website that allows users to search within the site.

search engine
A website used to search other sites for keywords.

social media
Forms of online communication in which people share content.

white space
The blank space on a page.